EMMANUEL JOSEPH

The Symphony of the Species, Music, Mind, and the Story of Human Connection

Contents

1

Chapter 1: The Dawn of Sound

From the rhythmic drumming of ancient tribes to the harmonious chants that echoed through early civilizations, music has been a cornerstone of human experience. It began as a primal call, a way to communicate and connect with others in a world that was still young and mysterious. Early humans used the sounds of nature as their first instruments – the rustle of leaves, the roar of the wind, and the song of birds. Over time, these natural sounds were mimicked and adapted, leading to the creation of the first musical instruments. Music became a vital part of rituals, celebrations, and daily life, acting as a universal language that transcended the barriers of spoken word.

The role of music in early human societies was multifaceted. It was not only a form of expression but also a means of survival. Rhythmic patterns helped coordinate group activities, such as hunting or building. Songs and chants carried the oral traditions and histories of communities, ensuring that knowledge was passed down through generations. Music also played a crucial role in social cohesion, bringing people together and fostering a sense of belonging and shared identity. As civilizations grew and evolved, so too did their musical traditions, reflecting the diversity and complexity of human cultures.

2

Chapter 2: The Birth of Harmony

As human societies advanced, so did their understanding of sound and harmony. The development of musical scales and the invention of new instruments allowed for more complex compositions. Ancient Greece, for instance, saw the emergence of theoretical frameworks for music, with philosophers like Pythagoras exploring the mathematical relationships between different pitches. This period marked the beginning of a more structured approach to music, where rules and conventions were established to create harmonious sounds. The idea of harmony, both in music and in society, became a central theme in human thought and culture.

Harmony in music mirrored the harmony sought in human relationships and communities. It represented balance, order, and beauty – ideals that were highly valued in many ancient cultures. The intricate melodies and harmonies created by early musicians reflected their aspirations for a harmonious world. Music became a way to explore and express complex emotions, thoughts, and ideas, providing a deeper understanding of the human experience. It was during this time that music began to be seen not just as an art form, but as a reflection of the human soul.

3

Chapter 3: The Sound of Civilization

With the rise of great civilizations came the flourishing of diverse musical traditions. In ancient Egypt, music was an integral part of religious ceremonies and royal courts. Instruments like the harp, lyre, and flute were used to accompany hymns and dances. Similarly, in Mesopotamia, music was a key aspect of temple rituals and celebrations. The spread of empires facilitated the exchange of musical ideas and instruments, leading to a rich tapestry of sounds and styles across the ancient world. Music became a symbol of cultural identity and pride, with each civilization contributing its unique voice to the global symphony.

The role of music in these ancient civilizations went beyond mere entertainment. It was deeply intertwined with their spiritual and social fabric. Temples, palaces, and public spaces resonated with the sounds of music, creating an atmosphere of reverence and celebration. Musicians held esteemed positions in society, and their skills were highly valued. Music also served as a means of education, with children being taught to play instruments and sing from a young age. The legacy of these ancient musical traditions can still be felt today, as they laid the foundation for the diverse and vibrant musical cultures that we enjoy.

4

Chapter 4: The Rhythm of Life

Throughout history, music has been a reflection of the human condition – its joys, sorrows, struggles, and triumphs. In times of war, music has been used to rally troops and boost morale, while in times of peace, it has been a source of comfort and solace. Folk songs and ballads have told the stories of everyday life, capturing the essence of human experiences and emotions. Music has also been a tool for protest and social change, giving voice to those who seek justice and equality. From the spirituals sung by enslaved people to the anthems of civil rights movements, music has been a powerful force for change and unity.

The rhythm of life is mirrored in the rhythms of music. Just as life has its ups and downs, music has its crescendos and diminuendos. The beat of a drum can mimic the heartbeat, creating a connection between the listener and the music. This connection is not just emotional, but also physiological, as music has been shown to affect heart rate, blood pressure, and even brain activity. The power of music to influence our physical and emotional states is a testament to its deep connection to the human experience. It is a universal language that speaks to the core of our being.

5

Chapter 5: The Dance of Cultures

The exchange of musical ideas and traditions between cultures has been a driving force in the evolution of music. Trade routes, migrations, and conquests have all contributed to the blending of musical styles and the creation of new genres. The Silk Road, for example, facilitated the exchange of instruments and musical techniques between Asia and Europe. This cultural cross-pollination enriched the musical landscapes of both regions, leading to the development of new sounds and styles. The fusion of different musical traditions reflects the dynamic and interconnected nature of human societies.

Dance has also played a crucial role in the development of music. The rhythmic movements of dance are intrinsically linked to the rhythms of music, creating a harmonious interplay between the two art forms. Different cultures have their own unique dance traditions, each with its distinctive rhythms and movements. These dances often tell stories and convey emotions, adding another layer of meaning to the music. The relationship between music and dance is a testament to the holistic nature of human expression, where sound and movement come together to create a complete artistic experience.

6

Chapter 6: The Melody of Innovation

Innovation has always been a driving force in the evolution of music. The invention of new instruments and the development of new musical techniques have expanded the possibilities of musical expression. The introduction of the piano in the 18th century, for example, revolutionized the world of music, offering a greater range of dynamics and tonal colors. Similarly, the advent of electronic instruments and recording technology in the 20th century opened up new horizons for composers and performers. These innovations have allowed musicians to explore new sounds and push the boundaries of what is possible in music.

Innovation in music is not just about technology, but also about creativity and experimentation. Composers and musicians have always sought to challenge conventions and explore new ideas. From the complex harmonies of Bach to the avant-garde compositions of John Cage, the history of music is filled with examples of innovative thinking. This spirit of exploration and experimentation is what keeps music vibrant and evolving. It is a testament to the endless possibilities of human creativity and the never-ending quest for new ways to express ourselves.

7

Chapter 7: The Harmony of Nature

Music has always been deeply connected to the natural world. Many musical instruments are made from natural materials, such as wood, metal, and animal hides. The sounds of nature have also inspired composers and musicians throughout history. The chirping of birds, the rustling of leaves, and the crashing of waves have all found their way into musical compositions. This connection to nature is a reminder of the deep bond between humans and the environment. Music is a way for us to celebrate and honor the beauty and wonder of the natural world.

The harmony of nature is also reflected in the rhythms and patterns of music. Just as nature has its cycles and rhythms, music has its own structure and form. The repetition of a melody or the steady beat of a drum can create a sense of order and predictability, mirroring the cycles of nature. This connection to nature is not just about aesthetics, but also about a deeper understanding of our place in the world. Music reminds us that we are part of a larger whole, connected to the earth and all its inhabitants.

8

Chapter 8: The Voice of the Soul

The human voice is the oldest and most natural instrument. It is a direct expression of our thoughts and emotions, capable of conveying a wide range of feelings and ideas. Singing has been a fundamental part of human culture since the dawn of time, used in rituals, celebrations, and storytelling. The power of the human voice lies in its ability to connect with others on a deep emotional level. A song can move us to tears, fill us with joy, or inspire us to action. The voice is a window to the soul, revealing our innermost thoughts and feelings.

The act of singing is also a form of self-expression and personal empowerment. Whether singing alone or in a group, the experience of using our voice to create music can be deeply fulfilling and transformative. Singing allows us to connect with our emotions and express our individuality. It also brings us together with others, creating a sense of community and shared experience. The human voice is a powerful tool for connection, capable of bridging the gaps between us and fostering a sense of unity and belonging.

9

Chapter 9: The Symphony of Emotions

Music has the unique ability to evoke a wide range of emotions. A piece of music can transport us to a different time and place, stir memories, and awaken feelings we may have forgotten. The emotional power of music lies in its ability to speak to the heart and soul, bypassing the intellect and reaching us on a visceral level. This emotional connection is what makes music such a powerful and universal form of expression. It allows us to communicate our deepest feelings and connect with others on a profound level.

The symphony of emotions that music evokes is a reflection of the complexity of the human experience. Just as life is filled with a mix of joy, sorrow, excitement, and tranquility, music can capture and convey these varied emotions. A minor key can evoke a sense of melancholy, while a major key can bring feelings of happiness and celebration. The dynamics of a piece – its loud and soft passages, its crescendos and diminuendos – mirror the ebb and flow of our emotional lives. Music has the power to move us, to touch our hearts, and to speak to our souls in a way that words alone cannot.

This emotional power of music is what makes it such a universal form of expression. Across cultures and throughout history, music has been used to express the full spectrum of human emotions. From the joyful rhythms of African drumming to the mournful melodies of Irish folk songs, music has the ability to transcend cultural boundaries and connect us on a fundamental level. It is a language that we all understand, regardless of our background or experience. The symphony of emotions that music evokes is a testament to its deep connection to the human condition.

10

Chapter 10: The Healing Power of Music

Music has long been recognized for its healing properties. From ancient shamans who used chants and drumming to heal the sick, to modern music therapists who use music to treat a variety of conditions, the therapeutic potential of music is well documented. Research has shown that music can reduce stress, alleviate pain, and improve mood. It can also enhance cognitive function and boost the immune system. The healing power of music lies in its ability to affect us on a deep, emotional level, tapping into our inner resources for healing and growth.

Music therapy has been used to treat a wide range of conditions, from anxiety and depression to Alzheimer's disease and chronic pain. The process of creating and listening to music can help individuals express their emotions, process their experiences, and connect with others. In a therapeutic setting, music can provide a safe and supportive environment for healing and personal growth. The benefits of music therapy extend beyond the individual, as it can also enhance social connections and improve the overall quality of life. The healing power of music is a testament to its profound impact on our well-being.

11

Chapter 11: The Future of Music

The future of music is filled with exciting possibilities. Advances in technology continue to revolutionize the way we create, share, and experience music. Digital platforms have made music more accessible than ever before, allowing artists to reach global audiences and fans to discover new sounds from around the world. The rise of artificial intelligence and machine learning is opening up new frontiers in music composition and production, enabling artists to experiment with innovative techniques and create entirely new genres.

As we look to the future, the role of music in society is likely to continue to evolve. Music will remain a vital form of expression and connection, reflecting the changing landscape of human experience. New technologies will provide opportunities for collaboration and innovation, while preserving the rich traditions of the past. The future of music holds the promise of endless creativity and discovery, as we continue to explore the limitless possibilities of sound.

12

Chapter 12: The Universal Language

In conclusion, music is a universal language that transcends cultural, social, and linguistic boundaries. It is a powerful force that has the ability to connect us, to heal us, and to inspire us. Throughout history, music has played a central role in human society, reflecting our deepest emotions and shaping our collective experiences. It is a testament to the enduring power of music that it continues to be a source of joy, comfort, and inspiration for people around the world.

The story of human connection through music is a testament to the resilience and creativity of the human spirit. Music has the power to bring us together, to bridge the gaps between us, and to create a sense of unity and belonging. It is a celebration of our shared humanity, a reminder of the beauty and complexity of the human experience. As we continue to create and share music, we are weaving a rich tapestry of sound that reflects the diversity and interconnectedness of our world. The symphony of the species is an ongoing story, one that will continue to evolve and inspire for generations to come.

Chapter 10: The Healing Power of Music

Music has long been recognized for its healing properties. From ancient shamans who used chants and drumming to heal the sick, to modern music therapists who use music to treat a variety of conditions, the therapeutic potential of music is well documented. Research has shown that music can reduce stress, alleviate pain, and improve mood. It can also enhance cognitive function and boost the immune system. The healing power of music lies in its ability to affect us on a deep, emotional level, tapping into our inner resources for healing and growth.

Music therapy has been used to treat a wide range of conditions, from anxiety and depression to Alzheimer's disease and chronic pain. The process of creating and listening to music can help individuals express their emotions, process their experiences, and connect with others. In a therapeutic setting, music can provide a safe and supportive environment for healing and personal growth. The benefits of music therapy extend beyond the individual, as it can also enhance social connections and improve the overall quality of life. The healing power of music is a testament to its profound impact on our well-being.

Chapter 11: The Future of Music

The future of music is filled with exciting possibilities. Advances in technology continue to revolutionize the way we create, share, and experience music. Digital platforms have made music more accessible than ever before, allowing artists to reach global audiences and fans to discover new sounds from around the world. The rise of artificial intelligence and machine learning is opening up new frontiers in music composition and production, enabling artists to experiment with innovative techniques and create entirely new genres.

As we look to the future, the role of music in society is likely to continue to evolve. Music will remain a vital form of expression and connection, reflecting the changing landscape of human experience. New technologies will provide opportunities for collaboration and innovation, while preserving the rich traditions of the past. The future of music holds the promise of endless creativity and discovery, as we continue to explore the limitless possibilities of sound.

15

Chapter 12: The Universal Language

In conclusion, music is a universal language that transcends cultural, social, and linguistic boundaries. It is a powerful force that has the ability to connect us, to heal us, and to inspire us. Throughout history, music has played a central role in human society, reflecting our deepest emotions and shaping our collective experiences. It is a testament to the enduring power of music that it continues to be a source of joy, comfort, and inspiration for people around the world.

The story of human connection through music is a testament to the resilience and creativity of the human spirit. Music has the power to bring us together, to bridge the gaps between us, and to create a sense of unity and belonging. It is a celebration of our shared humanity, a reminder of the beauty and complexity of the human experience. As we continue to create and share music, we are weaving a rich tapestry of sound that reflects the diversity and interconnectedness of our world. The symphony of the species is an ongoing story, one that will continue to evolve and inspire for generations to come.

Chapter 13: The Silent Symphony

Silence, often overlooked, plays a profound role in music and life. The pauses between notes, the rests in a melody, and the quiet moments of reflection all contribute to the overall impact of a musical piece. In the same way, silence in our lives allows us to pause, reflect, and appreciate the sounds around us. It provides a space for introspection and mindfulness, helping us connect more deeply with ourselves and others. The silent symphony of life teaches us that sometimes, the absence of sound can be just as powerful as the presence of it.

In music, silence is used to create tension and release, to emphasize certain notes or phrases, and to give the listener a moment to absorb and reflect on what they have heard. Composers and musicians understand the importance of these silent moments, using them to shape the flow and structure of their compositions. In our fast-paced world, silence can be a rare and precious commodity. Embracing moments of silence allows us to tune into the subtleties of life, to listen more carefully, and to connect more deeply with ourselves and those around us.

Chapter 14: The Digital Age of Music

The digital age has brought about a revolution in the way we create, share, and experience music. The internet and digital technology have democratized music production and distribution, giving artists from all corners of the globe the ability to reach audiences worldwide. Streaming services, social media platforms, and online communities have transformed the music industry, allowing for greater diversity and accessibility. The digital age has also fostered new forms of collaboration and experimentation, as musicians can now easily connect and create across geographical boundaries.

The impact of the digital age on music is evident in the rise of new genres and subcultures, the blurring of boundaries between different styles, and the increasing influence of technology on music creation. Electronic music, for example, has grown exponentially, with producers using software and digital instruments to craft intricate and innovative sounds. The ability to sample, remix, and mash-up existing tracks has led to a vibrant culture of musical experimentation. The digital age has also given rise to virtual concerts and online music festivals, bringing live music experiences to audiences around the world. The future of music in the digital age holds endless possibilities, as technology continues to evolve and shape the way we create and consume music.

18

Chapter 15: The Eternal Melody

As we conclude our exploration of music, mind, and human connection, it is clear that music is an eternal melody that weaves through the fabric of our lives. It is a universal language that speaks to the heart and soul, transcending time and space. From the ancient rhythms of our ancestors to the digital beats of today, music has always been a powerful force for connection, expression, and transformation. It is a testament to the resilience and creativity of the human spirit, a reflection of our shared humanity, and a source of joy, comfort, and inspiration.

The eternal melody of music reminds us that we are part of something greater than ourselves. It connects us to our past, our present, and our future, creating a sense of continuity and belonging. Music is a celebration of life in all its beauty and complexity, a reminder of the power of art to uplift and unite us. As we continue to create, share, and experience music, we contribute to the ongoing symphony of the species, a harmonious blend of voices that tells the story of human connection. The melody of music will continue to resonate through the ages, a timeless expression of the human experience.

The Symphony of the Species: Music, Mind, and the Story of Human Connection

In "The Symphony of the Species," embark on a captivating journey through the timeless relationship between music and the human experience. From the primal rhythms of our ancient ancestors to the digital beats of the modern era, this book explores how music has shaped and reflected our emotions, cultures, and connections.

Discover how the first sounds of nature inspired early humans to create musical instruments and harmonies that transcended language barriers. Delve into the birth of harmony and the role of music in ancient civilizations, where it was not just a form of entertainment but a crucial aspect of ritual, survival, and social cohesion.

Uncover the dance of cultures as music evolved through the exchange of ideas along trade routes and migrations, leading to a rich tapestry of sounds and styles. Explore the innovative spirit that has driven musical creativity, from the invention of new instruments to the rise of electronic music and digital technology.

Learn about the profound impact of music on our emotions and well-being, from its therapeutic properties to its ability to foster social connections and bring about social change. Finally, look to the future of music, where new technologies promise to continue revolutionizing the way we create, share, and experience sound.

"The Symphony of the Species" is a celebration of the universal language of music and its enduring power to connect us, heal us, and inspire us. Join this exploration of the melody of human life, and find yourself immersed in the harmonious blend of history, culture, and the human spirit.